MELODIES FROM THE CHAMBER

Words from The Inner Sanctuary

ROBIN AYSCUE

First Printing

Book Cover & Interior Design by Robin Ayscue
All Photographs including cover taken by Robin Ayscue

All Scripture is taken from the King James Version of The Holy Scriptures.

✿✝✿
ACKNOWLEDGEMENTS

To my Angel on Earth, *Ashley Hope*. Thank you so much for helping me finally complete this work. The formatting would have taken much longer without you! You as always are a constant source of encouragement and strength for my life and everyone who knows you. You are my forever angel. I love you with all of my heart and nothing will ever change that! Since my last book, we have also had a beautiful wedding with you as the gorgeous bride, now we can welcome *Brandon Cothran* to the family! All my love to both of you!

To my Mom, *Peggy Burnette*. Thank you for living your life in a way that makes me desire to know Christ. You are a living example to me of His Love and constant comfort. While I know that I am not the woman you are yet, I know that I have your continuous prayers to help guide me on my way. You are and always have been my best friend. I love you.

To my Extended Family who always offer their love, support and encouragement. My brother, *Steve Burnette,* and his sweet wife, *Kim*. My nieces and their families, *Amy* and *Joey Motz* along with *Shelby* and *Ben*. *Holly* and *TJ Williams,* along with *Caroline* and *Noah*. *Rebecca* and *Jarid Shaw* who just welcomed the newest member of our family, *Brielle Cara*. I don't know what my life would be without each one of you and I love you.

To my Uncle and Aunt, *Butch* and *Carol Caston*, thank you so much for your years of encouragement and support. I love you, *Binky!*

To my Aunt, *Lorene Burris*, thank you for your constant prayers for me through out the years. I love you too, *Binky!*

To *Mrs. Ruth Whitaker and Elaine Hill*, thank you so much for your love and prayers. Your encouragement and support mean the world to me. Thank you both for all your little notes while editing this work. I love you and couldn't have done it without you.

To You, *My Dear Reader*, thank you for taking the time to read these words. If they draw you at all closer to our sweet Savior, then they have accomplished their mission.

❧✝❧
DEDICATION

I wish I could take credit
For the words that you will read,

I wish somehow that I could say
That there's something here about me,

But my hand is just His Instrument
Guided across the page,

By His Blessed Holy Spirit
The beautiful words are His to say,

For I could never even think
What He so sweetly speaks,

My heart could never even conceive
The thoughts He brings to me,

So if somehow you are blessed
By the words you are to read -

Please give all Glory and all Praise to Him
For there is not one word here from me!

These words like all others are dedicated to the Love of my Life!
It is to the forever Lover of my Soul that this book is given.
May He receive all of the Glory for these words.
I love you with all my heart and soul Jesus,
I long for the day that my eyes finally meet Yours!

INTRODUCTION

Dear Friend,

WELCOME! Please come with me and visit a place beyond your dreams. A place that can only be found with your heart. You can search with all your mind and never find it. I am talking about an enclosed place deep down inside of you. The place where the Spirit of God dwells... The Chamber of Your Heart.

The following pages describe a holy, sacred, place to me. They are not mere words on a page but a life - altering experience, an experience I am humbled and honored to share with you.

The words in this book were actually written years ago. They started with 'The Chamber Writing,' and came rapidly over the next few weeks. Every time I felt His Spirit stirring and would pick up my pen a chamber poem would start to flow. I felt as though I literally lived inside this chamber during this time and I never wanted to leave. I began to feel the Lord lead me to create a power point version of these words with music and voice over to distribute. I tried to follow His instruction. All the words He whispers are always His to do with as He pleases. Finally the work was finished and ready to publish. It all came in a very even flow of His Spirit - from first poem to finished product was only 4 months. An outpouring of His Spirit!

Exactly 10 days after the work's completion my life and my family came under a spiritual attack unlike anything I had ever faced. I seemed to run from the chamber and try to get a grasp on all that was taking place as each day the stronghold of the enemy bared down harder. As the days progressed I lost all of the work that I had previously completed on 'Melodies From The Chamber.' Whether or not I could actually live in the chamber was being tried strong and true. I felt absolutely blindsided, out of nowhere these events one by one seemed to be coming to pass. Without question it was an all out attack of the enemy of our souls.

During this time there was one song that literally played in my soul all the time. I know you may not believe me but it did. During nights of lying awake crying all night, it sang. During fits of rage and anger at what the enemy was doing, it sang. During unrest, broken hearts, and tattered spirits, it sang. The music never stopped, all I had to do was stop the endless internal assault and listen. It was always playing and His Spirit was singing over me to bring me His Peace and Comfort. The name of that song was 'Thou, O Lord.' Our choir at church, of which I was a member, had recently learned it. The words of the song are taken from Psalm 3:1- 6. You know that I absolutely have to share them with you.

Lord, many are they increased that trouble me,
Many are they that rise up against me.
Many there be which say of my soul,
There is no help for him in God.
But Thou, O Lord, are a shield for me,
My glory and the lifter of my head.
I cried unto the Lord with my voice,
And He heard me out of His Holy Hill.
I laid me down and slept, I awaked:
For the Lord sustained me.

And sustain me He Did! All Glory and Praise be to God for His Unending Mercy and Grace, all involved came through. Changed? Yes. Stronger? Yes. Healed? Yes.

At times through the years I have gone back and read this sweet work. But always with a heavy heart attached to it of what it could have been. I felt that perhaps I had not passed His Test by cowering to the severe enemy attack. But oh my friend, His Tender Mercies are so gentle and sweet. With His Sweet Love He drew me back to these holy, sacred words and received me back into His Chamber. He had been waiting there with open arms of Mercy and Grace all along.

This time He has lead me to put these words into the form of a book for others to enter into this sacred place. How blessed it has been these weeks to tread on this hollowed ground. There is a season for all things and how grateful I am to Him that these words have birthed anew in my soul. You see I had to experience each word of this work before He allowed me to share it with you. I can testify to you that the joys of His Chamber are more glorious than anything in this life. My prayer for you is that you too will enter into this most glorious place and forever abide.

As we have revisited each verse, God has whispered new fresh words along with adding a few lines of a hymn. I have cried, sang, laughed and wished there was some way to hug God during this joyous time. It is quite humbling to hold a book in your hands with your name on it and know within your heart that you didn't write a word of it! All praise to our Magnificent King! Thank you so much for sharing this journey with me.

Not a moment is wasted when we kneel before the One whose story we long to tell, whose life we long to emulate, whose love we long to give.

If you have never entered into the depths of the Chamber of Your Heart, prepare for the experience of a lifetime!

THE CHAMBER WRITING

Come My People,
Enter thou into thy chambers
and shut thy doors about thee.
Isaiah 26:20

❧❦

We are almost at the chamber door. Do you hear the far-off distant music getting closer and closer? Are you starting to feel anticipation? Is your heart and mind excited at the thought of what lies beyond the door? Do you somehow know that after you enter, You will never be the same again? Do you hear the beautiful Voice of God calling your name? No other voice sounds so sweet! After you have answered the Call of This Voice, You will desire it every moment of every day. You will yearn for it, long for it, and do anything to please it from now on.

My favorite part of the next poem talks about the Creative Power that guides my hand across the page. 'His Spirit writes the words I say,' is so very true. For only He can create such a dream of beauty and have the power to express it to me. I ask that you would lay aside anything that would hinder you from approaching the beauty that awaits you inside the door. Maybe it is time, work, pride or lack of faith. Resolve it and find Him.

The Musical Prelude is beginning.

Listen with your heart…

Prepare to Enter His Chamber…

❧❦

The Chamber Writing

I close my eyes to go to sleep
But there's a yearning deep inside of me,
Sweetly, softly calling my name
His Voice inside me begins to raise,

Beckoning me to come to Him
Gently drawing me so deep within,
Inside this chamber I know so well
For this is where His Spirit dwells,

Such beauty my eyes begin to see
As His Words become alive in me,
His Voice strong, yet sweet He speaks
About the Love He has for me,

Inside this chamber no one else can see
The Creative Power that moves in me,
Guiding my hand across the page
His Spirit writes the words I say,

Inside His Arms I go to sleep
Inside this chamber where we do meet,
As He sweetly, gently, sings to me
My soul, in Him is now complete.

※ ✝ ※

THE CHAMBER OF MY HEART

The King hath
brought me into
His Chamber.
Song of Solomon 1:4

᯽

The bells are ringing. Do you hear them? I love the sound of chimes when you are entering a church. They evoke a reverent respect, Something missing in many churches of our day. Listen to them, they have yet to start a melody...now they are merely giving us a call. A call to worship. That's what Sunday Morning church bells do, they call us to enter in, to worship, to listen, to learn. We can hear them now as we are entering into the Presence of the King.

In our world there are many things clamoring for our attention. Cell phones, entertainment, sports, even hobbies, travel...on and on the list goes. But those things are not present here.

Here we find a quiet Holiness that drives us to our knees. Here inside this Stillness we find a Love so strong that we immediately respond to its Pureness. We have no choice but to bow, face down before the sheer Majesty of His Presence. The chimes begin to silence. We have found forever and now we will never want to leave. The Beauty of Who He Is silently falls around us as we are kneeled before Him. He draws us to our feet. With unseen words He adores us, Placing upon us His Robe of Righteousness. We come to understand in these first moments alone with Him that we are only here because of His Magnificent Grace. He will teach us here in His Chamber, He will love us, He will draw us to know Him deeper than we thought humanly possible. Heaven on earth is possible if we only believe. I believe that the true beauty of heaven will be the realization that we are in His Presence and that we *never* have to leave!

᯽

The Chamber of My Heart

Within the chamber of my heart
God writes a love song soon to start,
About the dreams He sees in me
And the future clear that's meant to be,

Inside the chamber where He dwells
I begin to hear the chimes of bells,
That are drawing me to a brand new place
Where I will finally get to touch His Face,

A bit of heaven I now can see
Within His Presence I'll always be,
For that is what heaven will mean to me
To be by His Side and never leave,

I can feel the beauty that is all around
As He places upon my head His Crown,
The one that means I belong to Him
And that forever we'll live in wedded bliss,

His Love Song plays with each beat of my heart
Inside this chamber where we never part,
Where His Love for me will always live
And the love we share will have no end!

❧❧

THE CHAMBER
LOVE SONG

I will Praise The Lord according to
His Righteousness: and will sing
Praises to the Name of
The Lord Most High.
Psalms 7:17

❧❧

One of the greatest parts about being in love with someone is the ability to just 'Be.' You don't have to talk or pretend to laugh. You can just be yourself. You are happy just to be together. You are fully accepted. No worries or insecurities. You are loved.

Our next chamber experience allows us to just bask in the Stillness of Who He is. Resting inside of His Love. Letting His Glory wash over us and looking upon His Beautiful Smile. His request to you and me is simply to 'Be' with Him. What a wonderful place for us to abide!

❧❧

I love the hymn, 'In The Garden.' I sing it to Him often in our times together. I don't sing well but He doesn't seem to mind. He almost always draws near to me as I offer Him my feeble praise. I love the phrase that begins the second verse. You know it...sing along with me.

'He speaks, and the sound of His Voice is so sweet the birds hush their singing...'

How sweet is His Voice when He gently calls your name. The tender sound of His Voice will be just the beginning of the sweet love song that we will hear inside His Chamber.

Let His Voice fall over you
in tender hushed tones…

The Chamber Love Song

I feel the yearning so deep within
Urging me to be with Him,
Deep inside me where we meet
And I can freely fall down at His Feet,
His Voice urgent or so it would seem
As He beckons me to come and meet,
His Desire for me would be so great
He's prepared for me this wonderful place,

A place that no one else can see
Its beauty so enraptures me,
That this is where my soul would dwell
Inside this place that I know so well,
It's silent except the sound of the wind
As He gently calls me to, 'Enter in,'
To come and sit with Him a while
And just bask within His Tender Smile,

Here I know His familiar Touch
I love Him oh so very much,
He lets me kneel on bended knee
As tears of joy fall upon His Feet,
It doesn't matter be it night or day
His Love within me remains the same,
As His Voice draws me the whole day long
It becomes my heart's only love song!

❧ ✝ ❧
THE PRAYER CHAMBER

The Lord is My Rock and
My Fortress, and My Deliverer,
My God, My Strength,
in whom I will trust.
Psalms 18:2

Have you ever wondered why God would allow the burdens that you have in your life? What kind of God would allow these things to happen to you and the people that you love? Dwelling inside The Prayer Chamber you will meet the God who works all things together for your good. God longs to be our Strength, our Fortress, our Rock and our Deliverer. There is only one way for God to be those things to us. It is for us to need those things from Him. God allows the weights of life to come to us so that we will seek Him and find Him. So that we can know Him and the Beauty of His Presence. That's how He works all things for our good. Finding Him in the middle of my crisis is the best moment of my trial. It is also the beginning of the end of it. When my heart finally starts crying out to Him, He immediately becomes My Strength inside my weakness, My Fortress inside my fear, My Rock inside my despair, and My Deliverer inside my battle! I promise, when you meet Him in your prayer chamber, He will become those things to you too!

❧❦

One of the first things that we naturally want to do when we come into God's Presence is to make things right with Him. We are humbled to be before One who is so great. Begging for His forgiveness comes easily. Before we go any further, why not take a few moments and cleanse your heart? You are safe inside His Chamber; no one else need know. After all, this is between you and Him. Then your heart can sing with mine in complete adoration:

Sweet hour of prayer, sweet hour of prayer that calls me from a world of care,
And bids me at my Father's Throne make all my wants and wishes known:
In seasons of distress and grief, My soul has often found relief,
And oft escaped the tempter's snare, By thy return, sweet hour of prayer.

The Prayer Chamber

Inside the chamber I come today
I fall down on my knees and begin to pray,
The Father's Love will meet me there
As my praises rise to His eager Ears,
How could One so Magnificent and Great
Meet me in this darkened place,
That becomes brilliant white as He enters in
And His Presence forgives my every sin,
The praise I sing begins to turn the key
And opens the door to this chamber in me,
Here His Heart will meet with mine
And for awhile I will be His Bride,
In my feeble, weakened state
If I could only live inside this place,
If I could just stay and never leave
And lift my voice in praise to Thee,
Outside the Stillness that I find here
Is a load so heavy I have to kneel,
Beneath the weight of the cross I bear
Maybe that's why You have placed it there,
To keep me down upon my knees
To cause my heart to lift praise to Thee,
To draw me here to this glorious place
Inside the chamber where You live each day.

꙰ ꙰

Now your heart is cleansed,
And you stand dressed in
His Robe of Righteousness!
You have spent the time necessary to
make your heart ready
to enter His Throne Room…
Take one more opportunity to thank Him
for His Unfailing Mercy and Grace.

꙰ ꙰

꙰ ꙰

⊰✝⊱
THE THRONE ROOM OF
THE CHAMBER

...For He hath clothed me with the garments of
Salvation, He hath covered me with
The robe of righteousness,
As a bridegroom decks himself with ornaments,
And as a bride adorns herself with her jewels.
Isaiah 61:11

⤜❧⤛

What is it that makes you think of God? Do you only come to God when you need Him? Do you only come when you are in a panic or have an emergency? Today we are going to enter the Throne Room of Grace where God requests that we come boldly! Please spend the time necessary in your heart's chamber to find this Holy, Sacred Place. You will not be disappointed. I can promise you that finding time to spend with God will no longer be a problem. Your problem will be finding enough time to spend with Him. You will never want to leave His Beauty once you find Him on The Throne! He is altogether Lovely!

⤜❧⤛

Today inside His Chamber we get a glimpse of His Glory. Our first overwhelming tidal wave of His Magnitude. We have no doubts about Him here. He is the Creator of all that we know, He can do anything. Nothing is impossible with Him. We believe. We are in complete awe of who He is. Our hearts join together as we joyfully, reverently proclaim:

Crown Him with many crowns, The Lamb upon His Throne,
Hark! How the heavenly anthem drowns all music but its own!
Awake, my soul and sing, Of Him who died for thee:
And hail Him as thy matchless King thro' all eternity.

Crown Him the Lord of Heaven! One with the Father known,
One with the Spirit through Him given from yonder glorious throne!
To Thee be endless praise, for Thou for us has died;
Be Thou, O Lord, thro' endless days, Adored and Magnified.

ôîíáîí

The Throne Room
Of The Chamber

Your time spent in the chamber
Will affect all that you do,
For the chamber is the place
Where God reveals His Plans to you,
Deep inside the chamber
Is where He lives and breathes in me,
It's the Throne Room of His Presence
And where I forever want to be,
It is where His Love Song lives
And the melody sounds so sweet,
As it plays inside the chamber
And I dance around His Feet,
Here is where He rules in Love
Here is where He speaks,
Here is where we share His Love
As He reigns inside of me,
Here inside the Throne Room
Is His Power and His Grace,
But it's His Love that draws me
To His Chamber each and every day!

ôîíáîí

"For God so loved the world that He gave
His only begotten Son that whosoever
believeth in Him should not perish
but have everlasting life."
John 3:16

Today He will teach us of His Sacrifice. When is the last time that you really looked at His Cross. Before we go any further, let's praise Him for His Glorious Gift. Take a few moments alone with Him and prepare your heart for what He longs for you to see. His Cross of Love.

Sing the words with me to this familiar hymn as many times as you would like:

> *On a hill far away stood an old rugged cross,*
> *The emblem of suffering and shame,*
> *And I love that old cross where the dearest and best*
> *For a world of lost sinners was slain.*
>
> *So I'll cherish the Old Rugged Cross*
> *Till my trophies at last I lay down,*
> *I will cling to the Old Rugged Cross*
> *And exchange it some day for a crown.*

❧✝❧
THE SACRIFICE OF THE CHAMBER

There is a difference in knowing about the Cross
and experiencing the Sacrifice that Love
made for you. Our visit to His Chamber today
will prayerfully allow you to learn
how great the Father's Love is for you.

The Sacrifice Of The Chamber

Here inside the chamber where His Love is all around,
    I know His peaceful current
        As the Joy of His Presence is found,

Here I feel His Gaze as He looks down on me,
    And the Light from His Face
        Draws me up from my knees,

Placed firmly on His Lap I can now look into His Eyes,
    And there I see The Father's Love
        That deep within them lies,

It wasn't the brilliant color of His Eyes that transfixed me,
    But the story deep inside of them
        Of my life that He can see,

For He is My Creator, He formed me in His Mind,
    He destined that I would live
        For this very moment in time,

He has drawn me to His Chamber to share His Love with me,
    To whisper to my soul
        And to set my spirit free,

He whispers things so sacred, So special and so sweet,
    That tears run down my face
        As He brushed them from my cheek,

His Destiny He shares with me, The life for me He's planned,
He asks if I will fulfill His Dreams,
Then He offers me His Hand,

There I see the nail print scar, The One He took for me,
The One that bought the right for me,
To sit here upon His Knee,

I couldn't help but touch it, where the Nail had been in place,
I knew one day I would see it,
When I met Him face to face,

As my hand touched the darkened scar
Now tender tears ran down His Face,
He said, "These are tears of joy,"
For now I could see the price His Love had paid,

Again He asked me if I would lay
My life down inside His Hands,
So I threw my arms around His Neck
And felt Him hug me back,

Now I will live inside His Tender Embrace
For I will never leave,
And anywhere that life may take me
I know He carries me,

Deep inside this chamber
Now wrapped secure from all life's harms,
Is where I will live forever
Completely enthralled inside His Arms!

THE BRIDAL VEIL OF THE CHAMBER

...And as The Bridegroom rejoices over the bride, so shall thy God rejoice over thee.
Isaiah 62:5

What is it that lies between you and your heart's groom? Many things can stop us from entering into the secret chambers of the Father's Heart. It can be a simple act of obedience or an unbelieving heart. God never requires anything of us that He does not reward. Sometimes we think that we have to wait until we get to Heaven to receive the gifts that He has for us. Acts of love that we thought went unnoticed on earth will be unbelievably rewarded at His Throne - there we will offer back to Him what He has so freely given. But each day the rewards of Who He Is await us here, many times going unseen. The greatest reward that we could ever hope to have in this lifetime is the Joy of His Presence. The all-consuming Power of the Almighty God is available to us every moment of every day. No matter what He asks of you, yield your all to Him. For He alone is Our Reward!

❧❧

Today we enter further into His Holiness. Are you coming to understand, as I am, that He is worth whatever He requires? Whenever He says, 'No,' it is out of nothing more than pure love, just as we protect our children by not letting them run into the street to get their ball when a truck is coming. The child does not understand but we see the danger. The child may get mad, pout, scream and wail, but we still protect our child. Why? Because we love them. My dear friend, He loves us so....even when we get mad, don't understand, shake our fist in anger...His Gentle Love is still there. Just dream with me of the glories of finally seeing Him, face to face. If you don't know this one, just try it and hum along...

Nothing between my soul and the Savior, Naught of this world's delusive dream,
I have renounced all sinful pleasure, Jesus is mine, there's nothing between,
Nothing between my soul and the Savior, So that His blessed face may be seen,
Nothing preventing the least of His favor, Keep the way clear! Let nothing between.

The Bridal Veil Of The Chamber

Today as I enter His Chamber,
I fall down at His Feet,
But there is something between us,
It's the veil that covers me,
There's no way for me to remove it,
For all brides have a veil,
But He quickly states, 'I'm holding it,'
That He longs to remove the veil,
There are things that stand between us, ways I must forget,
Sins that I'm committing with my every breath,
These things keep me from His Presence,
They stop me from entering in,
To the Joys of His Chamber,
To My Soul's Lover and Best Friend,
I'm already down on my knees,
Please show me where I've sinned,
Please forgive my shameful ways and wash away my sins,
A tender smile crossed His Face as His Eyes lit up the room,
My hands had finally dropped the veil,
Now my heart could receive My Groom,
Quietly He bent down, His Hands lifting the veil,
His strong Hand then lifted my chin,
And my heart began to swell,
With a love that I have never known,
A peace then flooded my soul,
For when my eyes finally saw His Face,
My breath He took away,
I couldn't believe I had held the veil
Since our wedding day,
For no joy the veil had given me
Could have ever replaced His Face,
Now He lifted me up from on my knees
And He took me in His Warm Embrace!

JOY INSIDE THE CHAMBER

Your Heart shall rejoice, and
Your Joy shall no man take from you.
John 16:22

Love is the one thing we are promised will live throughout eternity. It is the one thing that binds us to those who have gone before us and that will bind us to those we may leave behind one day.

When we have love, we have almost every other fruit of the Spirit. Hope, Peace, Fulfillment, Kindness, Belief, but most of all, we have Joy. When you are in love, your face glows. Your eyes light up when you even speak or hear the name of your Love. The Joy inside your spirit shows in everything that you do. Does the Joy of Your Heavenly Bridegroom show in your life today?

❧ ☙

Today we simply get to enjoy being with our Bridegroom. He will fill us with His Joy unspeakable and full of Glory. Join with me as we radiantly, joyfully sing...

Joyful, joyful, we adore Thee, God of glory, Lord of love,
Hearts unfold like flowers before Thee, Hail Thee as the sun above,
Melt the clouds of sin and sadness, Drive the dark of doubt away,
Giver of immortal gladness, Fill us with the light of day.

All Thy works with joy surround Thee, Earth and heaven reflect Thy rays,
Stars and Angels sing around Thee, Center of unbroken praise,
Field and forest, vale and mountain, Flow'ry meadow, flashing sea,
Chanting bird and flowing fountain, Call us to rejoice in Thee.

Joy Inside The Chamber

Such joy inside the chamber,
    Such beauty there to see,
For this is where my soul meets His
    In everlasting peace,

Here we are together
    In a Holy, Sacred, Place,
Here my eyes can finally see
    The Beauty of His Face,

Here I finally come to know
    The warmth of His Touch,
I hear His whispered Words of Love
    That means so very much,

Here my soul can finally know Him
    As He really is,
In all of His Power and Glory
    And His Perfection without sin,

For He is My Redeemer
    And my soul's only desire,
He is the Melody that flows through me
    Of which I never tire,

Such Love He stirs within my soul
    No other man could tell,
The Love He's birthed inside of me
    For His Touch I know so well,

He is my beginning
    And one day my end will be,
Forever in His Presence
    Where I will live eternally!

HAPPINESS INSIDE THE CHAMBER

And the Peace of God which passeth all understanding
shall keep your heart and mind through Christ Jesus.
Philippians 4:7

What is your definition of Happiness? Is it money, possessions, accomplishments? Do you have to have a certain relationship to ever be truly happy? Whatever your belief of happiness, it is bound deep inside your heart. That's where the chamber of your heart is also.

If you desire anything more than you desire to meet God in this most glorious place, you will never know the true happiness of His Chamber. God's desire for us is to be as carefree as a little child. We are His Children. When is the last time you jumped up and down for joy? Or felt giddy over finding a new flower? What about just standing in the rain and letting it wash over you? Let God become your definition of happiness and you will reap tremendous success.

As I stated earlier my niece and her husband had their first baby recently. Nothing it seems can melt a heart faster than that brand new little bundle. Pure joy and happiness! It is difficult for us as adults to think of ourselves as children. Yet, God the Father calls us His Sons and Daughters, His Children, Children of God. The happiness He reveals to us today is that of a Father delighting in His Child. Can you see His Smile as He beams with pride and joy over you? Let's make Him proud as we joyfully sing to Him the following....

My Father is rich in houses and land,
He holdeth the wealth of the world in His Hands
Of rubies and diamonds, of silver and gold,
His coffers are full, He has riches untold.
I'm a child of the King, a child of the King:
With Jesus my Savior, I'm a child of the King.

Happiness Inside The Chamber

Another day inside the chamber,
A place I'll never leave,
For here inside His Chamber,
I can see My King of Kings,
Here in all His Glory,
As He guides me day by day,
I bow before His Majesty,
He is The Truth, The Life, The Way,
Kneeling down before Him,
I can feel His Gentle Touch,
As His big, strong Arms enfold me,
And He tenderly picks me up,
The Hand that holds the Universe,
Touches me on my cheek,
Such tenderness inside His Eyes,
I can feel His Love for me,
He doesn't even speak a word,
As He sweetly looks at me,
And looking there inside His Eyes,
I see my life as He sees me,
Happy, carefree, like a child,
One in whom He's pleased,
Not one who's weighted down with cares,
That's not how His Love sees me,
For He is King over everything,
He is Lord of all the earth,
There is nothing too great for Him,
And inside Him I find my worth,
I will become the child I see,
Living inside His Eyes,
For my desire is to please Him,
Each day of my life,
Sweet and tender is the smile,
That comes across His Face,
How precious is the time I spend,
Inside this Sacred Place!

❧✝❧
EACH DAY INSIDE THE CHAMBER

Every Day will I Bless Thee:
And I will Praise Thy Name
forever and ever.
Psalms 145:2

❧❧

One of the biggest lessons that I have ever had to learn is that I cannot start my day without God. I am not a morning person, I can stay up all night but do not bother me in the morning... Quiet, please! Sometimes though it may be way over in the morning before I realize that I haven't taken time to seek God's Will for that day. He is so loving and patient with me. He is always allowing me to learn my constant need of Him. So I have finally gotten into the habit of not letting my feet hit the floor before I have spoken to the Lover of My Soul. Then I grab some fruit and nuts and 'My Bible Basket.'

My favorite spot to meet with Him is my back porch. We watch the birds eating and a calm sweet Stillness is always waiting for me there. Yes, I even have been known to go out there when it is snowing...that's what blankets are for! Everything about my whole day goes better! (Hope ya'll enjoyed my porch pictures!)

❧❧

Items for a Bible Basket:
Bible (of course!)
Current Journal or Notebook (always have to be ready!)
Jesus Calling (my favorite devotional, you get the idea.)
Bible Study Book (aka. Beth Moore)
Hymnal (we sometimes sing!)
Tissues (just in case, I usually end up crying!)
Note cards (in case He lays someone on my heart)
Lots of extra pens (I can never find one!)

Today, just pretend that you are on the porch with me, let's worship Him together and sing....

I serve a risen Savior, He's in the world today:
I know that He is living, Whatever men may say,
I see His Hand of Mercy, I hear His Voice of Cheer,
And just the time I need Him, He's always near.
He lives, He lives, Christ Jesus lives today!
He walks with Me and talks with Me,
Along life's narrow way,
He lives, He lives, Salvation to impart!
You ask me how I know He lives?
He lives within my heart!

Each Day Inside The Chamber

Today inside the chamber,
    He quickly speaks to me,
That each day I must enter in,
    And bow down upon my knee,
Not a single day can be wasted,
    The cost would be too great,
If I start my day without Him,
    I will encounter huge mistakes,
For now that I have found Him,
    Inside this chamber oh so sweet,
I must come before His Presence,
    For each day to be complete,
No matter what the day may hold,
    I must enter in,
To meet with my soul's lover,
    To speak with my best friend,
So long the enemy had kept me,
    From the place where we do meet,
But he has no power to sustain me,
    If I will just stay upon my knees,
So each day before I breathe a word,
    Before the sun will rise,
I will meet Him in my soul's chamber,
    And there He will open my eyes,
He will order the day's events,
    He will guide me on my way,
Then He will kiss me on my cheek,
    And carry me throughout the day,
And when the night is falling low,
    Inside the chamber we will abide,
And He will sweetly hold me close…
    Until the next sunrise!

꒰ঌ⚜�꒱

GIFTS INSIDE THE CHAMBER

How many times do you try to let your problems be bigger than God? By that, I mean that you try and work them all out by yourself. Prayer is only a last resort. I wonder how God must feel when He sees us carrying around weights that He never intended. The only reason that we have the problem is to find God in the middle of it. Maybe your problem has been brought on by your own sinful choice or someone else's. God still longs for you to find Him and receive His forgiveness of yourself and of others. He is more than able to resolve everything that we can find wrong in our lives. He graciously rewards those that diligently seek Him. Let's get ourselves out of the way and let God be God!

Praise Him with me and sing this song of adoration and faith...

I don't know about tomorrow, I just live from day to day,
I don't borrow from its sunshine, For it's clouds may turn to gray,
I don't worry o're the future, For I know what Jesus said,
And today I'll walk beside Him, For He knows what is ahead,

Many things about tomorrow, I don't seem to understand:
But I know who holds tomorrow, And I know who holds my hand.

He is altogether Lovely,
This is My Beloved,
And this is my Friend!
Song of Solomon 5:16

Gifts Inside The Chamber

Each day inside the chamber
Abiding in Him I am complete,
Be it morning, noon or evening,
I will worship at His Feet,

Each day inside the chamber
All my problems disappear,
For the Joy of His Presence
Is all that my soul can hear,

How can you have a burden
When kneeled before One so great,
For the sheer Glory of His Presence
Makes my problems run away,

For the great love inside His Eyes
Is all that my soul can see,
And all my problems become so small
When I am sitting at His Feet,

The Wisdom of the Universe
Rests within His command,
And yet, inside the Chamber,
He offers me His Hand,

Each day inside the Chamber
Only Heaven could be more real,
For life inside His Chamber
Makes earth seem so surreal,

The problems that all run away
Never come back to stay,
For the Strength of His Chamber
Demands they stay at bay,

I will never leave Him,
My heart will remain forever true,
His Heart has waited so long for me
Into His Presence I'm finally wooed,

Each day inside the chamber
I stand singing for My King,
Offering words of adoration
My life is what I bring,

His Presence is so consuming,
So tender and so sweet,
My heart will never leave Him
For He is My Everything!

❧✝❧
THE CHAMBER'S CROSS

Search me, O God, and know my heart,
Try me, and know my thoughts,
And see if there be any wicked way in me
and lead me in the way everlasting.
Psalms 139: 23-24

Have you ever looked beyond the Cross to the Person hanging there? Have you ever felt His Blood fall onto your skin? Have you ever really looked at Him and wished you hadn't sinned? The Cross we visit within the chamber is not a Cross on a far away hill. It's personal. How can we ever forget it?

❧❧

The Chamber's Cross

Today outside the chamber door I go to enter in,
But a tiny voice speaks to me to look back at my sin,
Turning back I can see the fun I used to have,
My eyes began to fill with greed,
My heart longed for what I had,
My sinful ways so quickly seemed to over power me,
How quickly my heart seemed to forget,
The precious time spent on my knees,
But then a Voice strong and clear,
Began to speak to me,
Lest I forget His Benefits,
He called me to Calvary,
There I saw Him as He was dying for my sin,
My heart began to break in two,
How could I ever betray Him,
As the blood drained from His body,
I heard Him speak my name,
He called me to come closer still,
And I will never be the same,
For looking down from on the Cross,

His Eyes burned into my soul,
A pain that all of heaven and earth,
Never could have foretold,
Tears and sweat mingled with Blood,
Poured down from His Face,
And as I stood there it dawned on me,
That He hung there in my place,
For as I looked into His Eyes,
My life I again could see,
Every bitter thought I'd had,
With every wicked deed,
Every wrong I had ever done,
Hung with Him on that tree,
And there I stood, His pain -filled eyes,
Looking down at me,
I begged Him to forgive me,
I begged Him to stop the pain,
I began to scream His Name aloud,
'Jesus, I'm so ashamed!'
When I lifted up my head,
I again stood at the chamber door,
I quickly turned the knob and entered in,
While He locked the door forevermore!

Today our song of thanksgiving comes at the end of our reading. What better song could we sing than this one…

What can wash away my sin? Nothing but the blood of Jesus,
What can make me whole again? Nothing but the blood of Jesus,

Oh, precious is the flow, that makes me white as snow:
No other fount I know, Nothing but the blood of Jesus.

❧❀❧

Proclaim this anthem with me as we boldly prepare to enter
His Chamber where His Armor always abides…

Onward Christian Soldiers, Marching as to war,
With the cross of Jesus going on before,
Christ, the royal Master, Leads against the foe,
Forward into battle, See His banner go!

Onward, Christian soldiers, Marching as to war,
With the cross of Jesus, Going on before!

At the sign of triumph, satan's host doth flee,
On, then, Christian soldiers, On to victory!
Hell's foundations quiver, At the shout of praise,
Brothers, lift your voices, Loud your anthems raise!

❧ ✝ ❧
THE ARMOR OF
THE CHAMBER

Has Satan ever tried to defeat you? Do you sometimes feel powerless against his endless assaults? If you have then you are going to love our visit to the chamber today. Not only do we have a victory ahead, we have a Living, Breathing, Victorious Champion living in our midst. He is our King of Kings and Lord of Lords! No more defeat for us! Get ready to put on your armor!

❧ ❧

Out of all of the words in this book, the next poem maybe one of my favorites. For years, I carried it in my Bible. Remember, I went through a fierce battle after receiving these words...they are powerful! I used to read it often before I went to bed at night and at the beginning of my porch time. Still I can feel His Spirit rise up in me when I read these words. Today's poem takes up 2 pages. I pray that they will bless and encourage you in the same way.

Put on the whole Armor of God
that ye may be able to stand
against the wiles of the devil.
Ephesians 6:11

The Armor Of The Chamber

Today as I enter His Chamber
All of hell begins to moan,
Demons run in terror
As I approach God's Throne,
Knowing they're defeated,
Their screams vibrate throughout hell,
As they run back to their weak leader
To report once again they've failed,
For they can see better than I,
The Power I kneel before,
His Majesty, The King of Kings,
The One who my sins bore,
They can see His Splendor and Glory,
They run from Him in fright,
They watch their evil, wicked scheming
Collapse within His Sight,
They know that once I've entered in
To the Splendor of The King,
That I'm protected against their plan
And any outcome it could bring,
For as I fall before His Throne
And declare His Righteousness,
He places the Armor of His Breastplate
Tight around my chest,
While I begin to stand up straight
He wraps my goings in His Peace,
He places upon my humble head
The Helmet His Blood bought me,

Within my hand a Sword so powerful,
The spoken Word of God,
Satan cannot stand to hear it,
For here, his battle is lost,
As all of hell groans in defeat
I stand strong before My King,
Wrapped secure in His Power and Might
All of Heaven stands with me,
Confident the battle's won
As the war rages on,
The Promises of God I do declare
As I stand before His Throne,
There the Spoken Word of God
Energizes My King,
As He delights inside my faith,
The victory is His to bring,
He uses the Words to build a fortress
Strong inside of Me,
And there I stand safe and protected
By the Power of My King,
Satan's darts will continue to fly,
For he is an avid foe,
But he was defeated at the Cross
So very long ago…
Here inside the Chamber,
As God's Word stands strong and true,
I turn to face my Savior
As He whispers, '*I love you!*'

᠅✝᠅

MUSIC FROM THE CHAMBER

Praise Ye The Lord,
Praise God in the Sanctuary,
Praise Him in the firmament
Of His Power.
Psalms 150:1

❧❧

Do you ever hear music in your heart and you don't know where it is coming from? Have you ever gotten up in the middle of the night and a song is just playing in your mind? Who do you think is singing to you? Where is the music coming from? I believe that music is one of the most powerful forces that God created. God's Word tells us that He inhabits our praise; now that's powerful! A song can lift your spirit when you are down. It can bring healing to a sore or broken heart. It can invoke memories that you would have otherwise never remembered. Today in our visit to the chamber we are going to hear just one of God's Love Songs to us.

❧❧

When we truly realize the power of praise to God, our life will change forever. Receiving His Promise to inhabit my praise makes my heart want to sing continuously. I want to feel His Presence and often times inside of praise I do. He is Worthy to be adored without end. He has saved me, redeemed me, washed my endless list of wrongs against Him away! He has fulfilled His Promise of Heaven for all eternity with Him. Each day He fulfills His Promise of never leaving me, never forsaking me, always loving me. My Friend, just think of all that He has done for you and I know that you too will have a song that Jesus gave to you! Please praise Him with me in the following hymn...

I have a song that Jesus gave me,,
It was sent from heaven above,
There never was a sweeter melody,
'Tis a melody of love,

In my heart there rings a melody,
There rings a melody with heavens harmony,
In my heart there rings a melody:
There rings a melody of love.

Music From The Chamber

Sweet music flows up from the chamber
Flooding all my mind,
Vibrating throughout my body
As His Heart keeps beat with mine,

Deep inside the chamber
Lives the Source of Music Himself,
The Eternal Song of Heaven
Inside my soul is where He dwells,

He is the Master Conductor
His downbeats fall like rain,
The symphony He plays within my soul
Plays day after passing day,

The music never goes away
It doesn't end with time,
As His Sweet Words flow through my soul,
And His Refrain guides all my life,

The sweet music from the chamber
Inside my soul may it forever live,
Until I'm face to face with My Savior
And my praises eternally will sing to Him!

ABIDING IN THE CHAMBER

And now, little children,
abide in Him...
I John 2:28

The definition of the word *Abide* means to, 'endure, remain, last or reside.' For us to abide in Christ is something to be learned even though we are already there. You see, inside the Chamber is where we endure, remain, and reside already. We just don't know it! God allows different situations in our lives to cause us to just want to 'Abide' with Him and never leave. Have you learned how to abide in your heart's chamber?

❧❧

When we abide with Him we gain the abundant rewards of who He is. Abiding in the chamber is where we learn His richest lessons. Waiting *with* Him, waiting *on* Him, longing *for* Him to work. We all are waiting on God for something. No one can say that every prayer they've prayed has been answered...we all wait on Him. Such treasures are to be found while waiting, such fresh sweet abiding. Today's visit to the chamber He will teach us how sweet it is to simply let our sorrows go and abide with His Sweet Consuming Presence. What are you waiting on God for? Share it with Him again and then release the outcome to Him and His Glory. Then let's just enjoy Him and abide in Him. I know that you know this song, let's sing it to him inside His Stillness as we just abide...

There's a peace in my heart that the world never gave,
A peace it can not take away,
Tho' the trials of life may surround like a cloud,
I've a peace that has come there to stay!
Constantly abiding, Jesus is mine,
Constantly abiding, Rapture divine,
He never leaves me lonely,
Whispers O so kind: "I will never leave thee,"
Jesus is mine!

Abiding In the Chamber

Deep inside the chamber
Is where you learn to abide,
Where your spirit learns to be at ease
And your mind learns to unwind,

For this is where His Spirit sweet
Whispers Words of Peace,
Their gentle, quiet current
Brings my aching heart relief,

Here I learn to trust His Touch
The gentle guiding of His Hand,
Swiftly moving, never rough
Even when I don't understand,

Here my soul learns to rest
A deep, abiding sleep,
Where unrushed words with peaceful tones
Comfort the depths of me,

Abiding is a glorious place
Where I simple rest upon His Breast,
And listen to His Heart of Love
Beating deep inside His Chest,

Inside the chamber where He does abide
His Patient Teachings - oh, so sweet,
He stirs my heart with love for Him
That makes me never want to leave,

For when my will is focused true
On my Savior, King of Kings,
Abiding deep inside the chamber
Is where my heart learns to sing!

❧✝❧

MORNING IN THE CHAMBER

Until the daybreak,
and the shadows flee away...
Song of Solomon 2:17

ஃ•ஒ

The most glorious time of the day is the stillness right before sunrise. As God begins to awaken the day absolutely nothing could be more beautiful! God longs to awaken our souls to Him in the very same manner each day. He wants to fill us with His Presence. That way, we can reap the blessings of the day that He has in store for us. Find the stillness of His Call each and every morning and watch the day awaken with Him.

ஃ•ஒ

Sunrise in the chamber after a sweet time of abiding. No matter what you are waiting for my sweet friend I want to assure you that a sunrise is coming! Sometimes God answers our prayers like a lightning bolt but most often they are answered like a sunrise. That way God can take all the time He wants to create the glorious setting in which He will answer us and be glorified. Brilliant colors start filling the sky and we are still frightened, afraid to believe He has answered. Slowly He blows us a kiss and the clouds drift into place. As His Love arrives with His Glorious Presence, the sun begins to slip into the sky. Dawn is here…Praise Him with me as these words refresh our soul…

Walking in sunlight , all of my journey,
Over the mountains, thro' the deep vale:
Jesus has said, "I'll never forsake thee,"
Promise divine that never can fail,

Heavenly sunlight, heavenly sunlight,
Flooding my soul with Glory divine:
Hallelujah, I am rejoicing,
Singing His Praises, Jesus is mine.

Morning In The Chamber

It's morning in the chamber
And the sun begins to rise,
The darkness runs from His Presence
And a tender smile lights up His Eyes,
Every color you can dream of
He paints across the sky,
With clouds that He blew into place
Across the horizon now they fly,

All the flowers in the garden
Just outside the chamber door,
Begin to lift their heads in praise
On this beautiful sun-drenched morn,
The birds have sung for hours…
Their song never silenced here,
The earth is welcoming another day
To know Him better still,

But here inside the chamber
My eyes can hardly wait,
To watch Him unfold the morning
And see what He will create,
The sun now peeks over the horizon
Shining fully on His Face,
What a beautiful way to start the day
Inside this chamber of His Grace!

EVENING IN THE CHAMBER

✂︎✝︎✂︎

He made darkness
His Secret Place.
Psalms 18:11

At the end of every day we should be offering God Glorious Praise for the life He has given us:

For breath to simply be alive,
For eyes to see the beauty of His Creation,
For ears to hear the songs of the birds,
For touch to know the love of a child's hand,
For smell to catch the scent of a rose,
For taste to enjoy His bountiful Harvest,
Evening inside His Chamber is a glorious place!

᷒◦᷒

Sing this to Him and have the most peaceful sleep ever…secure inside His Chamber:

There have been names that I have loved to hear,
But never has there been a name so dear,
To this heart of mine, As the Name Divine,
The precious, precious Name of Jesus,

Jesus is the sweetest Name I know,
And He's just the same as His Lovely Name,
And that's the reason why I love Him so,
Oh, Jesus is the Sweetest Name I know.

꧁꧂

Evening In The Chamber

It's evening in the chamber,
Outside the window, darkness falls,
A blanket of stars starts to appear,
As His Loving Voice begins to call,

A Calming Peace resides in the chamber,
As a harvest moon begins to rise,
Here My Savior and My Protector,
Says I am His and He is mine,

He makes the darkness His Dwelling,
Inside Him I feel no fear,
For the darkness obeys His Voice,
As He whispers, 'I am here,'

I am safe inside His Chamber,
No tormentors can I see,
For His Eyes still shine as the noon-day,
Although darkness is all about me,

His Eyes, His Voice, His Beauty,
His Majesty and His Grace,
Make evenings inside His Chamber
An absolutely glorious place!

꧁꧂

❧✝❧ TIME INSIDE THE CHAMBER

I will praise the Lord at all times,
His Praise shall continually
be in my mouth.
Psalms 34:1

❧❧

Time inside the chamber is never wasted. God is constantly drawing us, loving us and teaching us. He is an all-consuming Presence that is never out of our reach be it day or night. He is never too busy or too tired to listen to even the smallest prayer. So great is the Father's Love for us! Think of all the time that you waste on things that matter so little, entertainment, daydreaming, planning... Time with God has rewards that only eternity will see. Invest in Him today.

❧❧

Have you spent enough time inside His Chamber to understand the value of your moments being spent with Him? I used to live my life on fast forward, running from one thing to the next. Bible study, choir practice, ladies meetings, church three times a week...plus work and the task of being a single parent! Not counting outings with friends and family! I look back and I don't know how I did it all. There is absolutely nothing wrong with one thing that I listed here. However, I have learned to study the Bible with Him, sing songs with Him, pray for others with Him...There is a Stillness that can only be found inside of who He is and my heart is addicted to it. While raising my daughter I wanted church to be the hub of our life, but not at the sacrifice of a relationship with Him. Live as many of your moments as you can inside His Stillness. Let's worship him together, I know that your heart feels the same:

Jesus is all the world to me, My life, my joy, my all,
He is my strength from day to day,Without Him I would fall,
When I am sad to Him I go, No other one can cheer me so,
When I am sad, He makes me glad, He's my friend.

Time Inside The Chamber

Time inside the chamber
  Never comes to an end,
For every time I go there
  I find my souls best friend,

He is never too sleepy,
  Too busy or afraid,
To welcome me within His Arms
  Inside the chamber that He's made,

He is always there for me
  He knows my beginning and my end,
He knows every thought I think
  And yet, He calls me His Friend,

Times inside the chamber
  Are filled with the sweetest memories,
Of unrushed talks with tender smiles
  And all the blessings love can bring,

Of endless refrains where music plays
  In endless harmony,
Where He softly sings over me
  And promises to never leave,

So time inside the Chamber
  Is an endless Melody,
Of Promises yet to be fulfilled
  And endless memories!

✥✝✥
ALONE INSIDE THE CHAMBER

I am My Beloveds, and
His Desire is towards me.
Song of Solomon 7:10

❧❧

The Voice of God sounds like a melody when it rises up within you. Can you believe that the God of everything that you can see wants to spend time with you? Do you feel as I do, what am I to One who is so great? Usually we will spend time with someone to get to know them better. But God already knows more about you than you know about yourself! So why would He desire to be with us? God longs for us to learn of Him. He knows the blessings that He has for us if we will just find the time to be alone with Him.

❧❧

As I am writing this, it is raining outside. I love rainy days, they draw me into a certain kind of quietness. But even that does not compare to what He has for us inside His Chamber today. Alone with Him. He has brought us through many lessons to bring us to this one. That there is nothing like Him. That He is all sufficient, all knowing, all powerful, altogether lovely. Today we will see Him in His Beauty and find that all things beautiful flow from His Heart of Love.

Who can cheer the heart like Jesus,
By His Presence all divine?
True and tender, pure and precious,
O how blest to call Him mine!

All that thrills my soul is Jesus,
He is more than life to me,
And the fairest of ten thousand,
In my blessed Lord I see.

Alone In The Chamber

Alone with Him in the chamber
He is my soul's only desire,
To be with Him unending
Of His Sweet Presence I never tire,

To be alone with Him and no other
To hear Him quietly speak my name,
When His Voice calls to me
No other sounds the same,

For His Presence fills all my soul
No corner left unturned,
There's no hidden place where He abides
There's nothing about me to learn,

He dwells deep inside of me
For me to learn of Him,
For me to seek His Gentle Ways
And learn His Tenderness,

How can One who is so Great
Even think of me,
What value can I be to Him
When He is everything,

And yet, here I am with Him
In His Chamber so sublime,
This is how I will spend eternity
In His Presence so divine!

HEALING INSIDE THE CHAMBER

The Lord is nigh unto them
that are of a broken heart, and
saveth such as be of a contrite spirit.
Many are the afflictions of the righteous,
but the Lord delivered Him out of them all.
Psalms 34:18-19

When you are hurting, it may be difficult to find the chamber. You may find yourself wanting to run away from it instead of towards it. You may want to blame the pain you feel on the God who lives in your hearts chamber. But there is only one enemy of our souls. The only true healing that can be had is found inside the One who resides within the chamber. He is the only One who has already paid not only for your eternal salvation, but also for your pain, anger, guilt and shame. Give it all to Him and let the healing begin!

How sweet and tender His Mercies are to those whose hearts are sore. How marvelous for us to realize that no matter how deep our pain may be, He has already bore it for us. How He gazes with deep wells of love and compassion flowing from His Eyes to the very deepest part of your pain. What type of healing do you desire from Him, The Greatest of Physicians? Whether it be physical, spiritual, or a broken heart and spirit, He alone is the only One who can heal you. Inside His Chamber today, feel His Presence fall over your brokenness and gently mend you. Sweetly sing from a fresh wellspring these words...

Be still, my soul: the Lord is on thy side;
Bear patiently the cross of grief and pain;
Leave to thy God to order and provide;
In every change He faithful will remain,
Be still, my soul: thy best, thy heavenly Friend
Thro' thorny ways leads to a joyful end.

Healing Inside The Chamber

Healing rests inside the chamber
For those whose hearts are broke,

For those who have had the enemy
Bind them up in sinful yokes,

For those who cannot find their way,
For those who fail to see,

For those who forget to spend
The needful time upon their knees,

A Balm resides in the chamber
A healing Touch for hearts that are sore,

A soothing, peaceful comfort
For those stung by all life's scorn,

For the Voice of the Chamber
Lets the melody play once again,

As the God that resides in the chamber
Sings His Love Song over again.

❧ ✝ ❧
REST IN THE CHAMBER

Come unto me all ye that labor
and are heavy laden, and
I will give you rest.
Matthew 11:28

$\approx \circ \ll$

Has your heart ever been so sore that you thought you would never recover? Have you ever needed a place to go where you could just rest? Where you could forget about the past, the future, and maybe even the present? In His Chamber today you will find that place. Your soul will know a rest that is beyond mere sleep. Your mind will know a dream beyond anything you could dream. Your heart will know a love beyond any pain your heart could feel. Sleep well!

$\approx \circ \ll$

Today He has brought us to a place of rest. Not just any sleep or nap but true deep rest inside of Him. He cannot just give us peace…He is Peace! All peace in any given situation is always Jesus. If by now on our journey together you have not laid everything else aside, please do it now. He is able to handle all of your burdens and trials. Then enter into His Presence and let Him sing you to sleep. You will awake refreshed and renewed with a sweet smile on your face. Softly sing this to Him as you drift off…

There is a place of quiet rest, Near to the Heart of God,
A place where sin cannot molest, Near to the Heart of God,

O Jesus, blest Redeemer, Sent from the Heart of God,
Hold us, who wait before Thee, Near to the Heart of God.

Rest In The Chamber

Inside His Chamber I go to sleep
And feel His Presence all around me,
Gently holding me throughout the night
Knowing inside Him everything is all right,

His Peace falls like a gentle breeze
Causing my weary eyes to sleep,
His Eyes will watch me the whole night long
While He hums to me the sweetest love song,

And while I sleep He will cause me to dream
About the place that He has made,
A place where I will always be
Where the light of His Face will never fade,

There I will finally be His Bride
And He will give to me Eternal Life,
He died so I could be with Him
How I wish my dream would never end,

He brushes the hair from around my face
While letting me dream of this wonderful place,
He knows He'll make my dreams all come true
So He blows me a kiss and waits for the morning's dew.

❧ ✝ ❧
DREAMS COME TRUE
IN THE CHAMBER

The Lord is my strength and my shield,
and is become my salvation.
Psalms 118:14

❧❧

God has dreams for you that you have never even thought of dreaming. I would have never believed that one of His Dreams for me would have been to create this work that you are reading. The only way that He can share His Dream with you is for you to spend time in your heart's chamber. He has not shared anything with me that is not available to everyone who knows Him as Lord and Savior. Fulfill His Desires, His Hope, and His Dreams for your life. He created you on purpose with a divine destiny to fulfill.

❧❧

Inside His Chamber is the place where dreams all come true! Why did God design you and bring your world to life? What does He see in you that you do not see? What does He want you to have that you do not have? Deep inside His Chamber are all of the answers. The more you are with Him, the more He will share with you about His Plans for your present and future. He will show you why He allowed the things of the past. Remember He makes all things beautiful in His Time. I can promise you that no matter what His Dreams for you may be, there will not be one more beautiful than the one you are already having. He is our every dream come true! Nothing else that we can ever accomplish can compare to simply knowing Him and being in His Chamber. Let's just adore Him together:

What a fellowship, what a joy divine,
Leaning on the everlasting arms,
What a blessedness, what a Peace is mine,
Leaning on the everlasting arms,

Leaning, leaning, Safe and secure from all alarms,
Leaning, leaning, Leaning on the everlasting arms.

Dreams Come True
In The Chamber

Being with Him in the chamber
My heart can feel no fear,
For all I can see is glorious
When His Presence is so near,

His Heart is so Magnificent
Inside of Him I'll always hide,
He'll protect me from all enemies
As in His Spirit I do abide,

For my heart to be alone with Him
For Him to bring me to this place,
For me to come to understand
His Beautiful, Undying Grace,

Just living inside the chamber
As He wills each day to unfold,
And to share His Tender Mercies
And know His Sacred Love untold,

Yes, being alone with Him in the chamber
A life long dream finally comes true,
Abiding sweet within His Presence
How He longs for your heart too.

❧ † ❧
DIRECTION IN THE CHAMBER

Teach Me to do Thy Will, for Thou art my God,
Thy Spirit is good, lead me into
The land of uprightness.
Psalms 143:10

꙳⬥꙳

Are you so confused you don't know which way to turn? Life has so many options sometimes it's hard to know which one is right for you. One of the blessings of chamber dwelling is that God is always right there to provide you direction. He sees the beginning from the end and knows exactly which spot you were created to fill. Be Still and then Listen.

꙳⬥꙳

Inside His Chamber is clear and very detailed direction. It is found inside His Stillness. When we wait on God in expectation of what He is going to do, we are activating our faith. God longs to be believed, trusted. We don't want to be quiet or still when we need direction in our life. We want the answers. God wants our *fellowship*. He already knows the answer. If you need direction, find a place of total silence, run into His Chamber. He will answer you. Hum this along with me as we approach His Majesty:

When we walk with the Lord,
In the Light of His Word
What a glory He sheds on our way,
While we do His Goodwill,
He abides with us still,
And with all who will trust and obey,

Trust and obey, For there's no other way
To be happy in Jesus, But to trust and obey.

Direction In The Chamber

Inside the chamber I am never alone,
For He is always there residing on His Throne,
Each time that I decide to leave
A deep yearning always beckons me,
To stay and be alone with Him
To never leave and stay at peace,
For every weary anxious tide
That I may feel deep down inside,
Rolls away at the chamber door
For my heart has learned what's in store,
His Gentle Touch and Tender Smile
Welcome me just inside,
His Warm Embrace surrounding me
My anxious spirit feels at ease,
No trail stands inside His Grace,
No angry word or bitter face,
He makes the crooked places then go straight,
As He turns my face to the path He's made,
He's created such a perfect home
Inside His Chamber where I'm never alone,
Where His Spirit always give me peace
And where my heart in Him is made complete!

❧ ✝ ❧

THE PATH TO THE CHAMBER

He brought me forth also
into a large place.
Psalms 18:19

~◈~

What has God asked you to give up in order to enter His Chamber? Dwelling with Him will always require a sacrifice on your part. The larger the sacrifice, the larger the blessing. The best part of all is that He has already paid your sacrifice. He has made a way for you. He has designed the path that will draw you to His Chamber…His Home…His Dwelling…His Heart. Do whatever He asks of you. He will be worth it, I promise! Follow me on the beautiful path that He takes me on today.

~◈~

There is unbelievable beauty to behold inside His Chamber today. It is almost too Holy to approach. It is a life changing truth. His Sacrifice of Love for us was once for all. We only have to accept Him once to belong to Him. Yet, His Sacrifice is working everyday, all day. It is active at all times. That is the truth of our visit today. Prepare your heart to visit Him with me:

Search me, O God, and know my heart today,
Try me, O Savior, know my thoughts I pray,
See if there be some wicked way in me,
Cleanse me from every sin, and set me free.

Lord, take my life, and make it wholly Thine,
Fill my poor heart with Thy Great Love Divine,
Take all my will, my passions, self and pride,
I now surrender: Lord, in me abide.

O Holy Ghost, Revival comes from Thee,
Send a revival - start the work in me,
Thy Word declares, Thou wilt supply our need:
For blessing now, O Lord, I humbly plead.

The Path To The Chamber

Today on the way to the chamber
You took me along the way,
You said we would take a different path
That You had something to show me today,
Softly you took my tiny hand
And I felt Your Gentle Nudge,
A tender smile lit up Your Eyes
As my heart began to tug,
Outside the Chamber we would see today
We would walk around the walls,
Looking up into the Heavens
I could see the walls were so very tall,
But that's not what we're here to see
You have something else in mind,
Along the path we walk hand in hand
As the sun begins to rise,
It's morning in the garden
Just outside the chamber door,
All the flowers are lifting their heads
Your Glory is what they live for,
As we approach the chamber door
There is something I've never seen,
The door is covered in a thorny vine
To enter in will cause me much pain,
But just as my hand begins to reach
You placed Your Hand on mine,
My hand's protected inside Yours
Only Your Hand felt the thorns from the vine,
So every time I enter in
To the chamber where You stay,
I enter through the Blood You shed,
The Sacrifice You made,
Not only did you make the chamber
A beautiful place for me to be,
You paid the price, You endured the pain,
So that my heart would forever be free!

❧ † ❧
THE MELODY OF THE CHAMBER

For as the earth brings forth her bud, and as the garden causes the things that are sown in it to spring forth; so the Lord God will cause righteousness and praise to spring forth before all nations.
Isaiah 61:11

Has your heart heard the song of your inner sanctuary yet? Can you sing along with the ever present melody of the chamber? Do you know your heart's score as it plays inside your soul?

If you are brokenhearted… it will sing,
If you feel despair… it will sing,
If you are grieving…. it will sing,
If you are confused…it will sing,
If you are joyous… it will sing,
If you are exuberant…it will sing,

Decide today that you will hear the melody of the chamber each day for the rest of your life.

❧❀❧

Today as we end our journey together, Let's lift this last song of complete adoration to Him:

There's within my heart a melody,
Jesus whispers sweet and low,
Fear not I am with Thee, Peace, be still,
In all of life's ebb and flow,

Jesus, Jesus, Jesus, Sweetest name I know,
Fills my every longing, Keeps me singing as I go!

The Melody Of The Chamber

Listen for the beautiful music
That's playing in your soul,
Let it fill all your being
As it gives you joy untold,

Let it draw you to His Chamber
The place where He does abide,
Let its melody fill your spirit
Until you're at peace deep down inside,

Then as your heart begins to Praise Him
The chamber door will slowly open,
And you will enter into His Beauty
And know Him as you've never known Him,

You will see His Radiant Glory,
You will feel the Beauty of His Face,
Your Heart will sing with His forever
As your heart dwells in this glorious place,

Don't let the music ever silence,
Let it forever play in your soul,
So that the Melody of His Calling
Will be all that your heart can know!

❧ ❦
A Final Note

Dear Friend,

Thank you so much for sharing this journey to your heart's chamber with me. I am beyond humbled that you have shared these sacred words also. I pray that you will always hear the song that God is singing over you.

Perhaps you have read these words and you can only think of the word chamber in terms of the prison you live in. My Friend, He has come to set you free! Maybe you have never met Jesus in the personal way described in this book. Maybe you didn't realize that you could experience a walk with Him day by day as these words have described. Please allow me a few moments to share how you too can know Jesus Christ as your personal Savior.

1. God wants us to experience His Peace and Love.
John 3:16 says, "For God so loved the world that He gave His Only Begotten Son that whoever believes in Him shall not perish, but shall have eternal life."

That 'Whoever' means anyone, no matter what they have done.

2. We are not and cannot automatically be at peace with God. We are by nature born into the world as sinners.
Romans 3:23 says, "For all have sinned and fall short of the Glory of God.'

The 'All' in this verse means all of mankind, every person ever born is born with a sin nature separating us from the Holiness of God.

3. God's Love was so great for us that it bridged the gap between us and Him. He sent His only Son, Jesus to die for our sins. He paid the price, took the penalty for our wrongdoing on the cross, three days later He rose again over coming death and the grave.

I Peter 2:24 says, "Who His own self bare our sins in His own body on the tree, that we, being dead to sins, should live unto righteousness: by whose stripes ye were healed."

4. You become a member of God's Family when you cross the bridge of His Love and accept Jesus by personal invitation.
John 1:12 says, "But as many as receive Him to them He gave the right to become the Children of God, even to those who believe on His Name."

To receive Jesus as your Savior you only need to do four things:

1. **ADMIT** your spiritual need. "I am a sinner."

2. **REPENT** and be willing to turn from your sin.

3. **BELIEVE** that Jesus Christ died for you on the cross.

4. **RECEIVE**, through prayer, Jesus Christ into your heart and life.
In Revelation 3:20 Jesus says, "Behold, I stand at the door and knock, if anyone hears My Voice and opens the door, I will come in."
Romans 10:13 says, "Whoever calls upon the name of the Lord, shall be saved."
Just pray this simple prayer:
Dear Lord Jesus, I know that I am a sinner and need Your Forgiveness. I believe that You died for my sins. I now invite you to come into my heart and life. I want to trust and follow you as Lord and Savior. In Jesus Name, Amen

My sweet friend, if you prayed that prayer then you have received the gift of eternal life and received Jesus as your personal Savior. I am so thrilled for you and want to hear all about it. Please contact me on the website and tell me about your decision. I also encourage you to start reading your Bible in the book of John. Find a good Bible believing church and start attending. Let the pastor know of your decision and He should be able to help you on your new walk. Praising God with you!

LIST OF HYMNS USED IN
MELODIES FROM THE CHAMBER

1. **In The Garden,** *by Charles A. Miles*
2. **Sweet Hour Of Prayer,** *by William Walford*
3. **Crown Him With Many Crowns,** *by Matthew Bridges*
4. **The Old Rugged Cross,** *by George Bennard*
5. **Nothing Between,** *by Charles Tindley*
6. **Joyful, Joyful, We Adore Thee,** *by Henry Van Dyke*
7. **A Child Of The King,** *by Harriet E. Buell*
8. **He Lives,** *by Alfred Henry Ackley*
9. **I Know Who Holds Tomorrow,** *by Ira Stanphill*
10. **Nothing But The Blood,** *by Robert Lowery*
11. **Onward Christian Soldiers,** *by Sabine Baring-Gould*
12. **There Rings A Melody,** *by Elton M. Roth*
13. **Constantly Abiding,** *by Anne. S. Murphy*
14. **Heavenly Sunlight,** *by Henry J. Zelley*
15. **Jesus Is The Sweetest Name I Know,** *by Lela B. Long*
16. **All That Thrills My Soul,** *by Thoro Harris*
17. **Be Still, My Soul,** by *Jean Sibelius*
18. **Near To The Heart Of God,** *by Cleland B. McAfee*
19. **Leaning On The Everlasting Arms,** *by Elisha A. Hoffman*
20. **Trust and Obey,** *by John H. Sammis*
21. **Search Me, O God,** *by J. Edwin Orr*
22. **Jesus Is The Sweetest Name I Know,** *by Lela B. Long*

If you have enjoyed this book
please feel free to visit with me
and let me know of your heart's song at:
www.robinayscue.com

*May You Always Hear
The Melody of Your
Heart's Chamber!*

To Order More Copies:
www.robinayscue.com
or find the author on Amazon.

COMING IN 2014
Secret Places Of The Heart

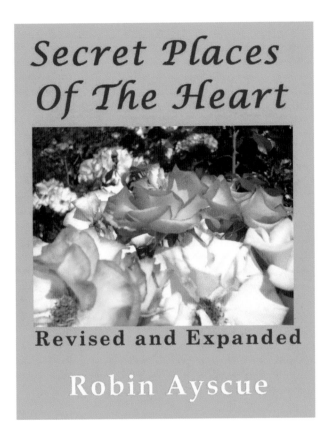

Robin Ayscue
978-1493615612

  If you enjoyed 'Secret Places of the Heart' previously, you will love the new revised work coming in 2014. The author has lovingly gone back through these words from over 10 years ago and added new insight.

  Come along with me to a place where we all want to live. You will find encouragement in a secret place of hope. Find calm in a place of peace. Receive happiness in a place of joy. Meet fulfillment in a place of love and destiny in a place of prayer. All of this is yours to enjoy in:

   "Secret Places Of The Heart"

Made in the USA
Charleston, SC
23 January 2014